How to Make a Treadle-operated Wood-turning Lathe

Designed by Bob Ingham
Written and illustrated by ApT Design
and Development (from original text)
and illustrations by Paul Smith

Step-by-step instructions on how to build and use a treadle (foot) operated lathe to turn wooden items such as bowls, chair and table legs and ornamental lamp bases.

Practical
ACTION
PUBLISHING

Practical Action Publishing Ltd
The Schumacher Centre
Bourton on Dunsmore, Rugby,
Warwickshire CV23 9QZ, UK
www.practicalactionpublishing.org

© Intermediate Technology Publications 1986.

First published 1986\Digitised 2013

ISBN 10: 0 946688 16 8
ISBN 13: 9780946688166
ISBN Library Ebook: 9781780442419
Book DOI: http://dx.doi.org/10.3362/9781780442419

Since 1974, Practical Action Publishing (formerly Intermediate Technology Publications and ITDG Publishing) has published and disseminated books and information in support of international development work throughout the world. Practical Action Publishing is a trading name of Practical Action Publishing Ltd (Company Reg. No. 1159018), the wholly owned publishing company of Practical Action. Practical Action Publishing trades only in support of its parent charity objectives and any profits are covenanted back to Practical Action (Charity Reg. No. 247257, Group VAT Registration No. 880 9924 76).

Acknowledgements

Financial assistance in the development of this lathe as well as in the production of this book was made available through the Intermediate Technology Development Group from a grant from the Overseas Development Administration (UK). Their assistance is gratefully acknowledged.

Introduction

This booklet describes the construction of a lathe for woodturning. It can be made from channel, angle and hollow steel sections, the sizes of which can be altered to suit local availability. The design also uses several bicycle components:

  Rear wheel with free wheel sprocket
  Chain
  Bottom bracket with crank shaft and ball bearings
  Pedal cranks and sprocket
  Inner tube
  Lower rear frame members.

The tools required are a drilling machine, electric welder and general hand tools such as files, hacksaw, engineer's square and G-clamps. The headstock pulley and the tailstock centre are most easily made with a metal-turning lathe, but can be made without one.

The lathe described in this booklet is a useful addition to any woodwork shop, enabling new products to be made without the use of electricity. With the lathe, decorative shapes can be put onto household items such as bowls, chair legs and lamp bases, and onto functional parts such as dowels and pulleys for other equipment, e.g. net making machines, weaving looms etc.

The type of machine described here is of course not the only way to approach low-cost, self-build wood-turning, but is offered as one way of meeting a widespread need.

Glossary

8mm clearance hole = hole through which the threads and shank of an
            8mm bolt can pass freely
Fig. 1   = Figure 1
$\varnothing$ = Diameter
M12   = 12mm Metric thread
MS   = Mild steel

Weld here   =

Contents

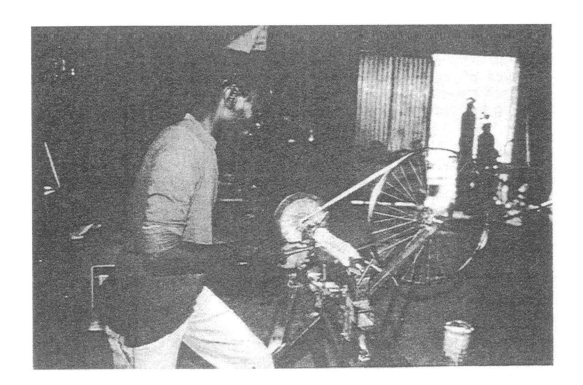

Uses of the lathe

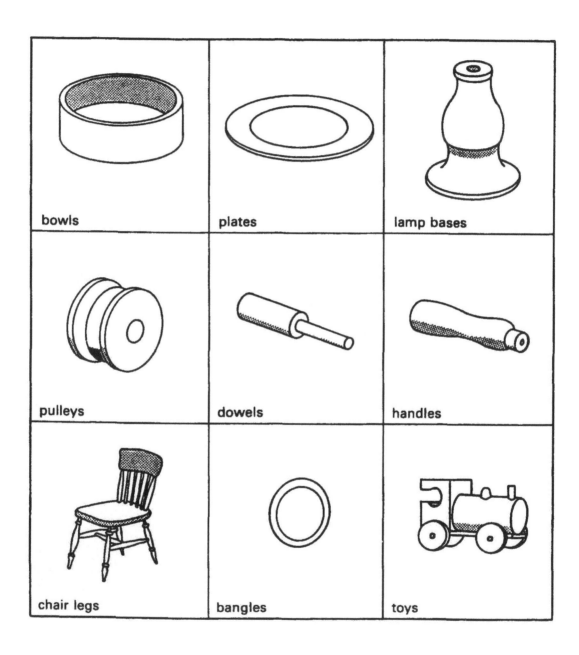

bowls	plates	lamp bases
pulleys	dowels	handles
chair legs	bangles	toys

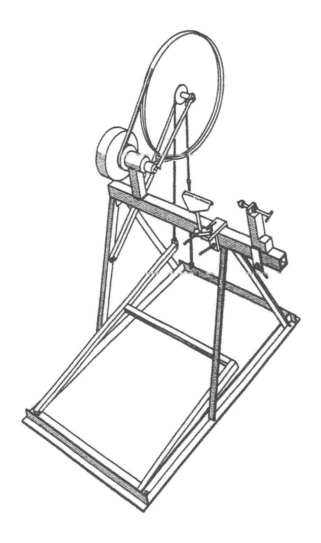

Figure 1 Complete treadle operated wood-turning lathe

6

Components of the lathe

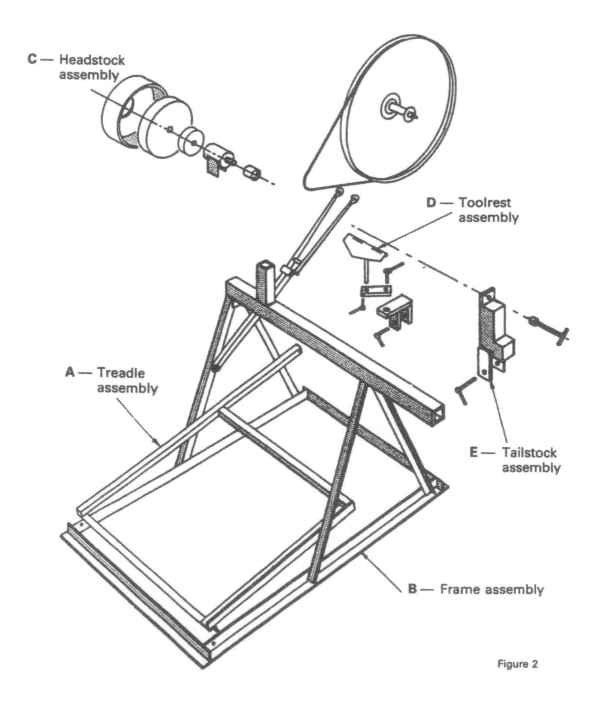

C — Headstock assembly

D — Toolrest assembly

A — Treadle assembly

E — Tailstock assembly

B — Frame assembly

Figure 2

Construction

TREADLE ASSEMBLY — A
PARTS

Part	Name	Quantity	Dimensions (mm)
A1	Foot bar	1	618 × 25 × 25 MS Angle
A2	Pivot angle	1	662 × 25 × 25 MS Angle
A3	Right side angle	1	735 × 25 × 25 MS Angle
A4	Left side tube	1	1185 × 25 × 25 MS Square hollow section
A5	Pivot pins	2	Ø10 × 60 MS Bar
A6	Chain	1	1200 Length of cycle chain
A7	Rubber strips	5	700 × 5 Rubber inner tube

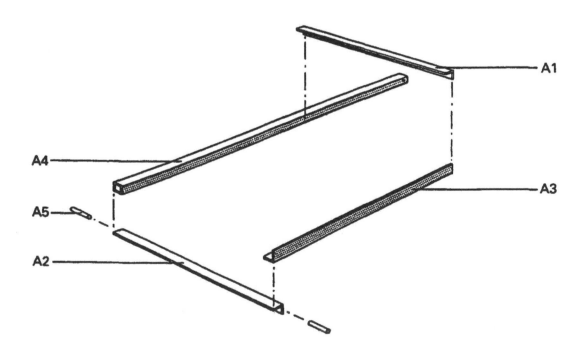

Figure 3

Weld one pivot pin **A5** to each end of the pivot angle **A2** as shown in Fig. 4. Drill a 3mm diameter hole at one end of the left side tube **A4** (Fig. 5). Clamp and weld the frame together as in Fig. 5, making sure that the corners are square and that the frame is flat before welding.

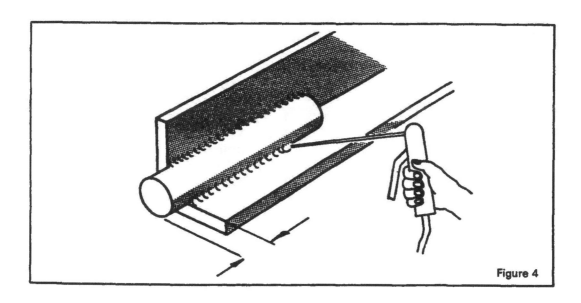

Figure 4

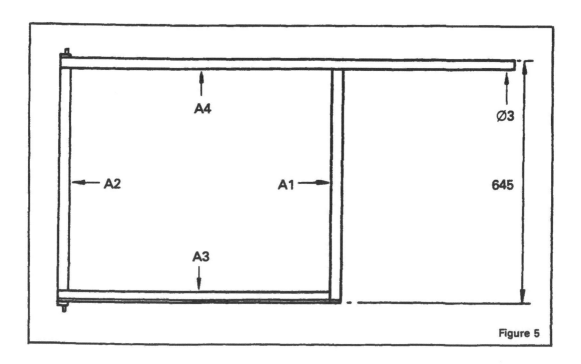

A4

Ø3

A2

A1

645

A3

Figure 5

FRAME ASSEMBLY — B
PARTS

Part	Name	Quantity	Dimensions (mm)
B1	Base angles	2	765 × 50 × 50 MS Angle
B2	Base side angles	2	1205 × 50 × 50 MS Angle
B3	Legs	4	945 × 50 × 50 MS Angle
B4	Top angles	2	75 × 50 × 50 MS Angle
B5	Cross brace	1	1040 × 25 × 25 MS Angle
B6	Main beam	1	1025 × 50 × 50 MS Square hollow section
B7	Headstock support	1	120 × 50 × 50 MS Square hollow section
B8	Forks	1	Lower rear frame members
B9	Angle	1	72 × 40 × 40 MS Angle
B10	Arm	1	440 × 50 × 50 MS Square hollow section
B11	Stays	2	560 × Ø8 MS Bar
B12	Cycle wheel	1	To suit Forks B8

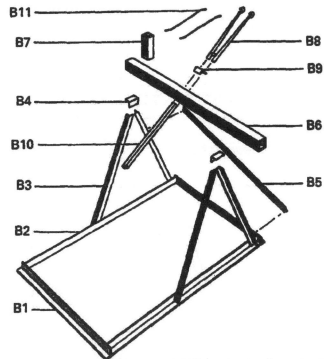

Figure 6

Clamp the base angles **B2** together and drill a 10mm diameter hole through both, as shown in Fig. 7. Assemble the angles **B1** and **B2** as in Fig. 8, with the treadle assembly in place, located by the pivot pins. Tack weld the corners. Check for squareness and then weld fully.

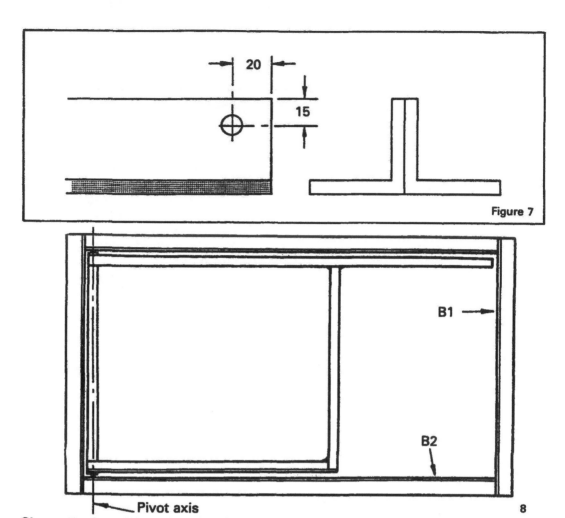

20

15

Figure 7

B1 →

B2

← Pivot axis

8

Clamp the legs **B3** to the base in the positions shown in Fig. 9. Clamp the top angles **B4** to the legs.

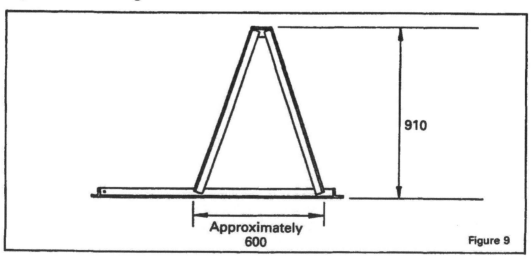

910

Approximately
600

Figure 9

11

Make sure that the top angles are parallel with the base side angles **B2**; clamping the main beam **B6** to the top angles across the frame will help with this alignment. Position the main beam with the left end level with the side angles, and overhanging on the other side (Fig. 10 — treadle not shown for clarity). Tack weld all the pieces in place, then weld fully.

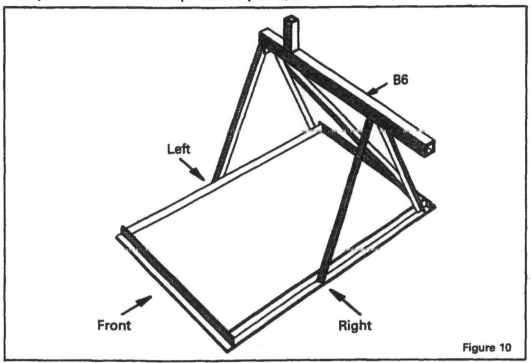

Figure 10

Note: Fig. 10 also indicates the front, left and right of the lathe for future reference.

The forks **B8** are cut from a bicycle frame or can be fabricated from angle iron. If angle iron is used, slots must be made to hold the wheel spindle, so that the drive belt tension can be adjusted. If a bicycle frame is available, cut as shown in Fig. 11.

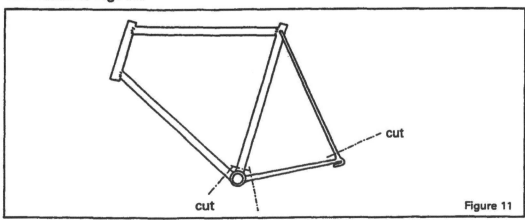

Figure 11

Weld the forks to angle **B9** (Fig. 12; see also Fig. 6).

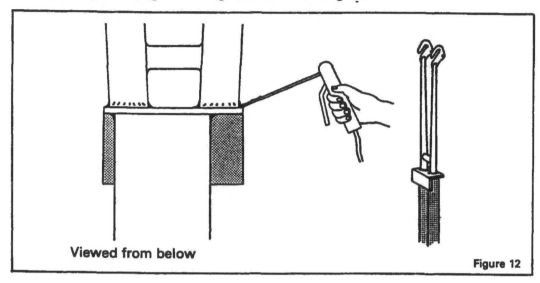

Viewed from below

Figure 12

The arm **B10** can be made from square hollow section or from two pieces of angle iron welded together. Position the angle **B9** and arm **B10** as shown in Fig. 12, and weld in place. Clamp the arm **B10** to the inside of the left side legs **B3**, so that the wheel centre will be positioned approximately as shown in Fig. 13. Weld the arm to the legs. Note that the wheel will be located to the rear, and on the left of the lathe.

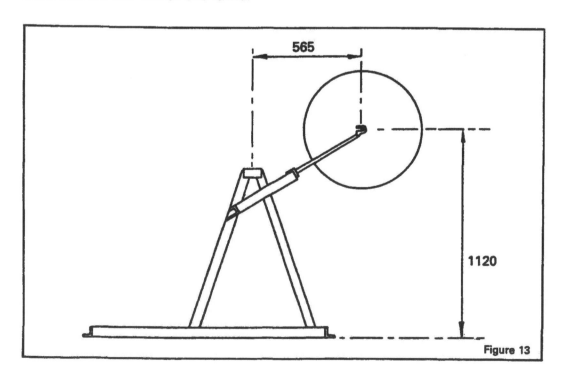

565

1120

Figure 13

Weld the headstock support **B7** to the main beam **B6** so that its centreline is approximately 40mm to the right of the centre of the cycle wheel **B12** (Fig. 14).

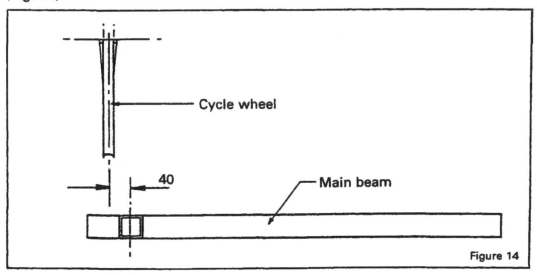

Figure 14

The stays **B11** can now be bent and welded so that they run from the outside of each fork to the main beam on either side of the headstock support (Fig. 15).

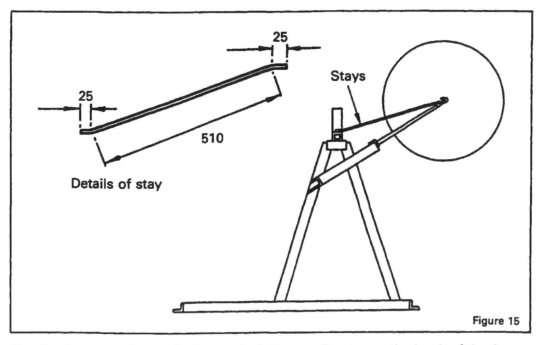

Figure 15

Finally, the cross-brace **B5** is welded diagonally across the back of the frame legs. This makes the frame rigid. Note that it is higher on the left to allow room for the treadle to rise and fall.

HEADSTOCK ASSEMBLY — C
PARTS

Part	Name	Quantity	Dimensions (mm)
C1	Flywheel	1	Approx. Ø200 (8 inches) brake drum
C2	Flywheel block	1	Approx. Ø160 × 35 Wood
C3	Chainwheel sprocket	1	Approx. Ø190
C4	Pulley	1	Ø80 × 15 Alloy
C5	Work support	1	Ø30 × 30 MS Bar
C6	Centre pin	1	Ø3 × 15 MS Bar
C7	Support pins	2	Ø4 × 24 MS Bar
C8	Bottom bracket assembly	1	
C9	Bottom bracket plates	2	70 × 50 × 2 MS Sheet
C10	Grub screw	1	M4 × 10

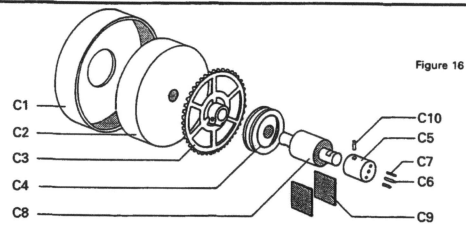

Figure 16

An old vehicle brake drum of approximately 200mm diameter is used as the flywheel **C1**. The wooden flywheel block **C2** should be cut to fit freely inside the flywheel (approximately 160mm diameter). Drill six holes (3mm diameter) through the flywheel. Centralise the block inside the flywheel and clamp it in position whilst pilot holes are drilled for six wood screws. Screw the flywheel and flywheel block together (Fig. 17).

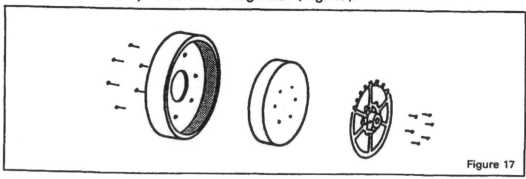

Figure 17

15

Saw off the pedal crank from the chainwheel sprocket **C3**, leaving the 'cotter pin' hole intact (Fig. 18). Drill six holes (3mm diameter) through the chainwheel sprocket to take wood screws. (It may be necessary to weld a piece of sheet metal to the chainwheel sprocket to take these screw holes if the 'spokes' are too thin).

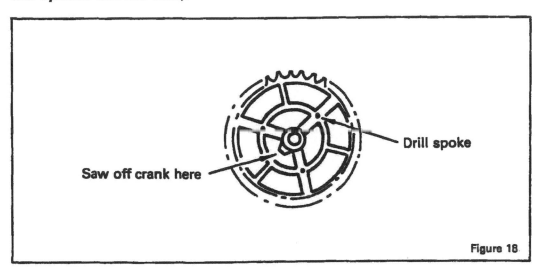

Drill spoke

Saw off crank here

Figure 18

Position the chainwheel sprocket **C3** centrally on the flywheel block **C2** and clamp in place. Drill three pilot holes through the holes in the chainwheel sprocket into the block. Screw the two components together with three screws only. Mount this flywheel on the spindle of the bottom bracket assembly **C8** and rotate it to check that the flywheel 'runs true'. If it runs very roughly, remove the screws and reposition the block on the chainwheel. When the flywheel runs smoothly, fit the remaining screws (Fig. 17).

Trim the excess material from the bottom bracket **C8** (Fig. 19).

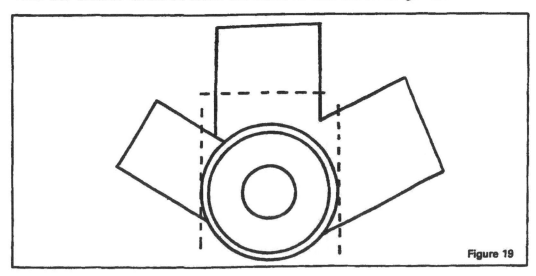

Figure 19

Remove the spindle and bearing cups. Cut the two plates **C9** and weld them to the bottom bracket (Fig. 20). Protect the internal threads while welding, by pressing a damp cloth inside the bottom bracket body. After welding, remove the cloth.

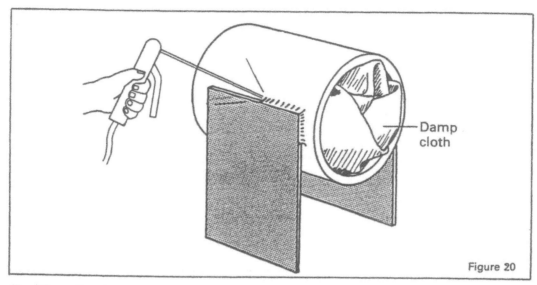

Figure 20

Position the bottom bracket on the headstock support **B7**, aligning the bottom bracket with the main beam by the following procedure: insert a straight piece of pipe or flat bar through the centre of the bottom bracket. Support the pipe or bar with wooden blocks placed on the main beam so that the bottom bracket is suspended with the plates **C9** against the headstock support **B7**. Check that the pipe or bar runs parallel to the main beam lengthways and vertically (x = y, Fig. 21). Clamp the plates to the headstock support and weld in place. Clean and grease the internal threads, then grease and refit the spindle and bearings.

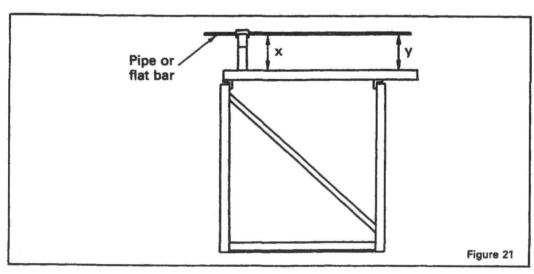

Figure 21

If a metal-turning lathe is available, the work support **C5** should be turned and drilled as in Fig. 22. Drill the large centre hole to fit the crank shaft. The support pins **C7** should be a press fit in their holes. The points can be filed after the pins have been pressed in. Drill and tap the work support to receive the M4 grub screw **C10**.

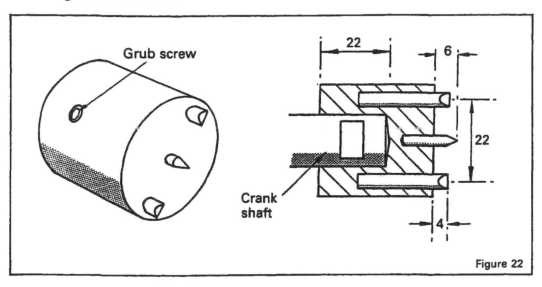

Grub screw

Crank shaft

22

6

22

4

Figure 22

If a metal-turning lathe is not available, cut off the other pedal crank, as shown in Fig. 23. Weld to this a washer and a short length (10mm) of 30mm diameter MS bar. Drill the bar and fit the support pins **C7** as in Fig. 22. In either case, mount the work support assembly on the spindle and rotate it to locate the centre. Mark and drill the centre, and fit the centre pin **C6**. Again, this should be a press fit in its hole; the point can be filed once the pin is in place.

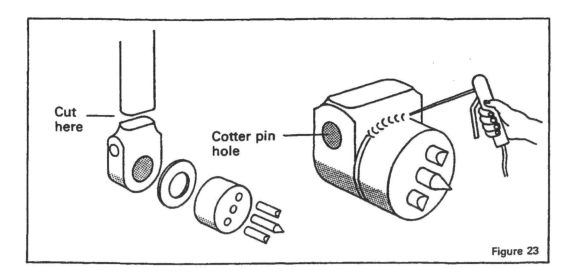

Cut here

Cotter pin hole

Figure 23

If a metal-turning lathe is available, turn a pulley to the dimensions shown in Fig. 24. The central bore should be drilled so that the pulley fits closely onto the crankshaft. Drill and tap the holes as shown in Fig. 24. If a lathe is not available, obtain a suitable pulley and adapt it to fit the crankshaft. The recess can be made by drilling and chiselling.

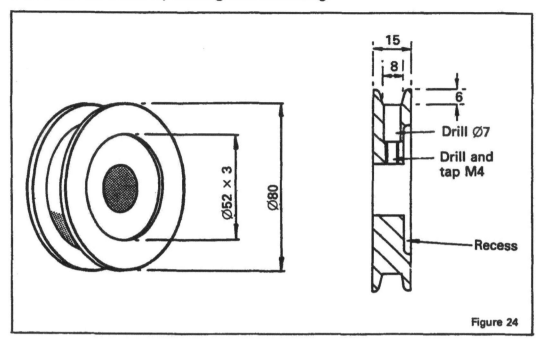

Figure 24

19

TOOLREST ASSEMBLY — D
PARTS

Part	Name	Quantity	Dimensions (mm)
D1	Upright	1	⌀12 × 145 MS Bar
D2	Tool support	1	200 × 64 × 1.6 MS Sheet
D3	Support bar	1	⌀12 × 200 MS Bar
D4	Adjustment plate	1	108 × 25 × 12 MS Flat
D5	Support bar lock	1	M6 Nut, M6 × 30 Bolt
D6	Thumb bar	1	⌀8 × 65 MS Bar
D7	Adjustment plate lock	1	M8 Nut, M8 × 30 Bolt
D8	Thumb bar	1	⌀8 × 65 MS Bar
D9	Saddle top plate	1	90 × 50 × 12 MS Flat
D10	Saddle side plates	2	64 × 38 × 6 MS Flat
D11	Saddle lock	1	M10 Nut, M10 × 75 Bolt
D12	Thumb bar	1	⌀8 × 65 MS Bar

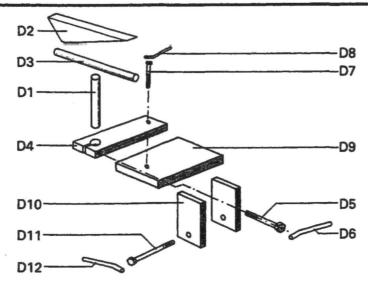

Figure 25

Cut out the tool support **D2**, according to Fig. 26, and put a slight bend across it as indicated.

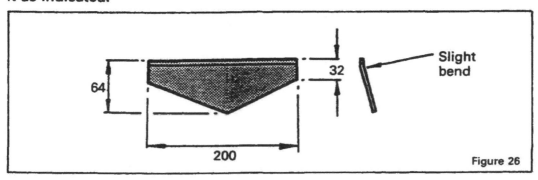

Figure 26

20

Weld together the upright **D1** and the support bar **D3** in a 'T' shape. Weld the tool support to the support bar (Fig. 27).

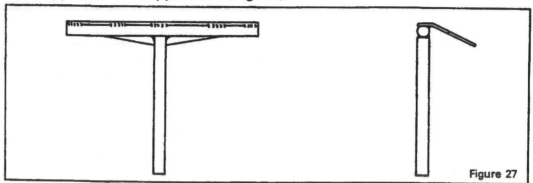

Figure 27

Cut and drill the adjustment plate **D4** according to the dimensions shown in Fig. 28. Put an M6 bolt through the hole and weld the nut in place. Take care not to weld the nut to the bolt.

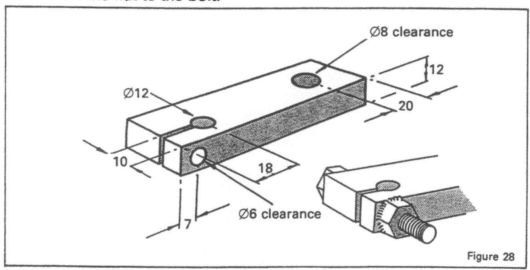

Ø8 clearance

12

Ø12

20

10

18

7

Ø6 clearance

Figure 28

The thumb bars **D6, D8** and **D12** should be bent and welded to their bolts **D5, D7** and **D11** (Fig. 29).

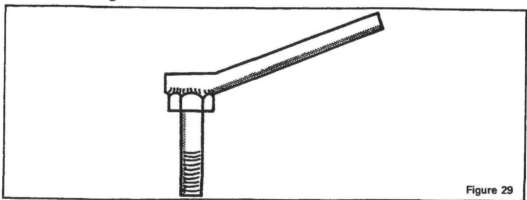

Figure 29

Drill the saddle top and side plates **D9** and **D10** as indicated in Fig. 30. Grind the side plates **D10** at 'V' (Fig. 31) so that the welds will not touch the main beam when assembled. Clamp the side plates to the main beam, placing a piece of thick paper on either side of the main beam to allow for a clearance (Fig. 31). Clamp the top plate in position and weld it to the side plates. Remove the paper and slide the saddle assembly fully down over the main beam. Check that the saddle lock bolt **D11** will pass through the holes in both saddle side plates. Again, put on the M10 nut and weld in place, as shown in Fig. 31. Similarly, weld the M8 nut on the saddle top plate. Assemble the whole toolrest and tighten all the locks.

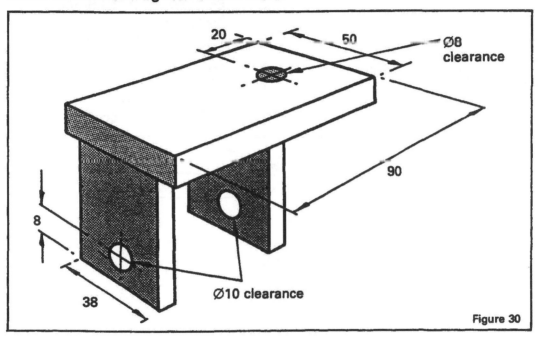

Figure 30

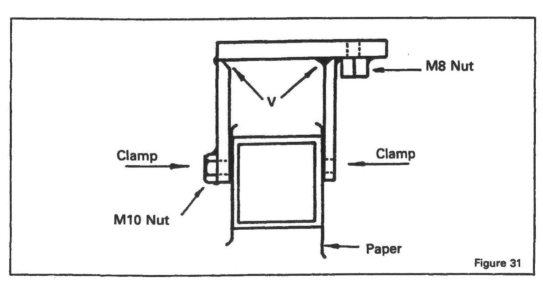

Figure 31

TAILSTOCK ASSEMBLY — E
PARTS

Part	Name	Quantity	Dimensions (mm)
E1	Work centre	1	Ø18 × 17 MS Bar
E2	Nuts	4	M10 Nut
E3	Adjusting bolt	1	M10 × 70 Bolt
E4	Thumb bar	1	Ø8 × 95 MS Bar
E5	Adjuster support	1	50 × 40 × 12 MS Flat
E6	Spacer tube	1	85 × 50 × 50 MS Square hollow section
E7	Saddle top tube	1	95 × 50 × 50 MS Square hollow section
E8	Saddle side plates	2	90 × 50 × 6 MS Flat
E9	Clamp bolt	1	M10 × 75 Bolt
E10	Thumb bar	1	Ø8 × 85 MS Bar
E11	Drive cord	1	11.5m Braided cord

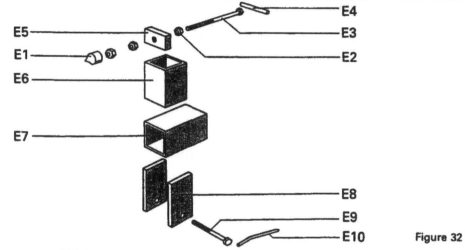

Figure 32

The work centre **E1** should be turned approximately to the shape shown in Fig. 33. Weld an M10 nut **E2** centrally to the work centre. If a lathe is not available, weld the piece of Ø18 MS bar centrally to the M10 nut. Screw the adjusting bolt **E3** into the nut, hold the bolt and rotate it whilst grinding the work centre until the shape shown is achieved.

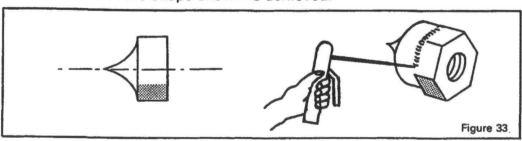

Figure 33

Weld the thumb bar **E4** to the head of the adjusting bolt **E3** (Fig. 34).

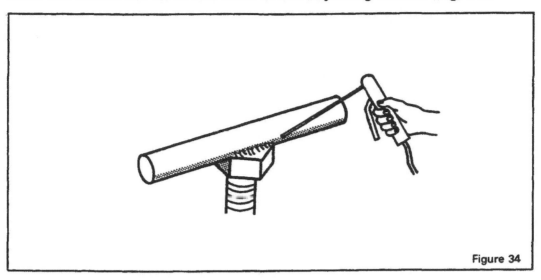

Figure 34

Drill a 10mm diameter hole centrally in the adjuster support **E5**. Weld this to the spacer tube **E6**. Cut the spacer tube **E6** so that the distance 'z' in Fig. 35 equals the distance from the top of the main beam to the centre pin on the headstock assembly. Weld the spacer tube to the saddle top tube **E7**. Weld an M10 nut **E2** onto the adjuster support, clamping it in place with a bolt whilst welding (Fig. 35).

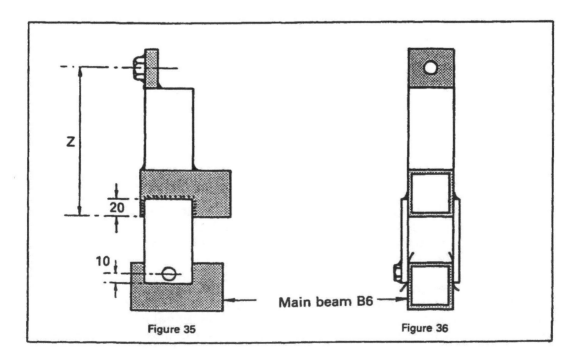

Z

20

10

Main beam B6

Figure 35

Figure 36

24

Drill 10mm clearance holes in the saddle side plates **E8** and weld an M10 nut **E2** over one of the holes. Clamp the plates to the spacer tube **E6** in the position shown in Fig. 35. Put a piece of thick paper in between each saddle side plate and side of the main beam to allow for a clearance (Fig. 36). The M10 nut must be on the saddle side plate at the back of the machine, when faced with the headstock on your left, and the tailstock on your right. Weld the tops of the saddle side plates to the spacer tube. Remove the clamps and paper.

Weld the thumb bar **E10** to the clamp bolt **E9** (Fig. 29). Screw this through the saddle side plates and **M10** nut. Screw a nut **E2** onto the adjusting bolt **E3**, and then screw the adjusting bolt through the adjuster support **E5** and into another M10 nut **E2** and the work centre assembly.

Assembly

Slide the pulley **C4** (with the recess towards the bottom bracket) onto the left end of the crankshaft until it is just clear of the bottom bracket. With a scriber, mark the shaft through the pulley locking-screw hole. Remove the pulley and file a small 'flat' on the shaft (Fig. 37).

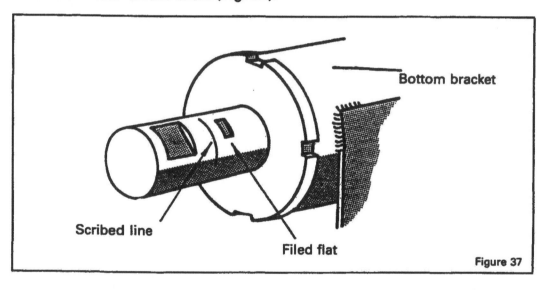

Bottom bracket

Scribed line

Filed flat

Figure 37

Replace the pulley and tighten the lockscrew onto the 'flat'. Slide the flywheel assembly onto the shaft and fit the crank cotter pin. Slide the work support onto the other end of the shaft and tighten the **M4** grub screw onto the cotter pin flat (see also Fig. 16).

Spin the flywheel by hand and mark the top of the flywheel when it stops. Repeat this several times. If the chalk marks appear in the same place each time (and the bearings are 'free-running'), then the wheel is out of balance. To compensate for this, put a lump of clay on the inside of the flywheel, where the chalk marks are. Spin and mark the flywheel again, repeating the process of adding or subtracting clay until it is balanced (Fig. 38).

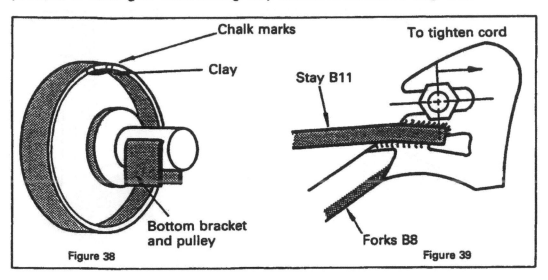

Figure 38

Figure 39

Remove the tyre and inner tube from the cycle wheel **B12**. Fit the cycle wheel into the forks with the sprocket on the left, and lightly tighten the wheel nuts with the wheel as near to the main beam as possible (Fig. 39). Wrap the drive cord **E11** around the cycle wheel and pulley in a continuous run five times, and knot the two ends together in a reef knot (Fig. 40).

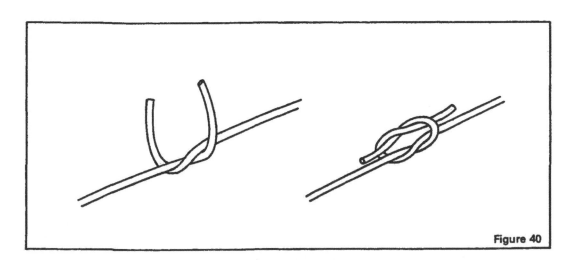

Figure 40

Slacken the cycle wheel nuts and move the wheel back until the cord loop is tight (Fig. 39). Tighten the wheel nuts. Attach the chain **A6** to the treadle by means of a 3mm wire or rod (Fig. 41). Take the chain over the sprocket and fit another wire hook on the other end. Fit a third hook to the base frame, through a hole drilled in the rear base angle **B1** in line with the sprocket. Join the two free hooks with strips of inner tube **A7**; alter the length of the strips to adjust the height of the treadle in the 'up' position (Fig. 42).

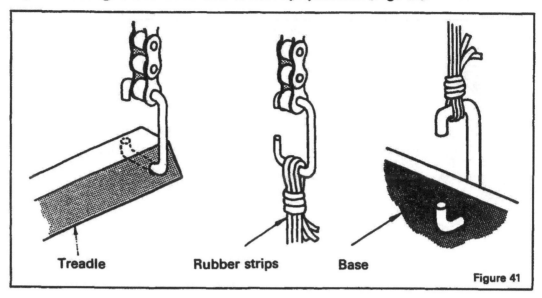

Treadle   Rubber strips   Base

Figure 41

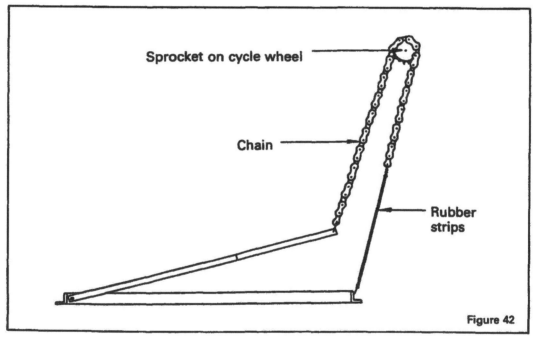

Sprocket on cycle wheel

Chain

Rubber strips

Figure 42

Fit the toolrest and tailstock assemblies onto the main beam.

Operation

When turning a long piece of wood (the 'workpiece'), the grain of the workpiece should run lengthways between the headstock and the tailstock; this prevents splitting across the grain. Mark the centres on the workpiece in pencil at both ends. Chisel or saw off the corners to make initial turning easier (Fig. 43).

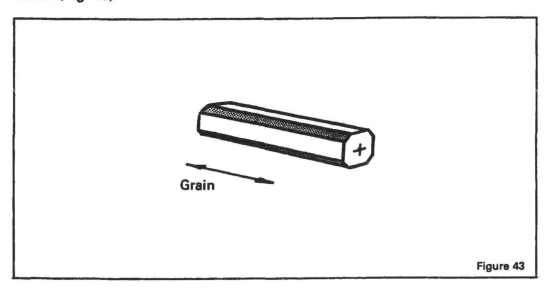

Grain

Figure 43

Spike the centre at one end of the workpiece on the headstock centre, then slide the tailstock along the main beam to spike the other centre. Tighten up the saddle clamp, screw up the adjusting bolt, and tighten the lock nuts (Fig. 44).

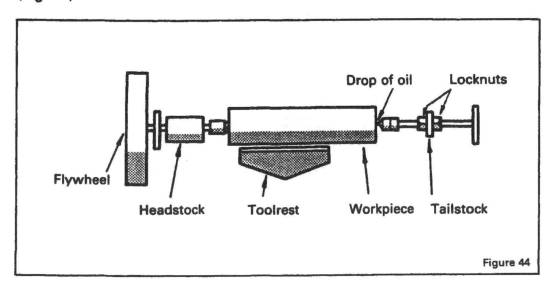

Drop of oil   Locknuts

Flywheel

Headstock   Toolrest   Workpiece   Tailstock

Figure 44

Bowls and other articles which cannot be held 'between centres' must be screwed to a 'mounting flange'. This can either be turned on a metal lathe, or fabricated by welding a piece of 5mm plate to a sawn-off pedal crank (Fig. 45).

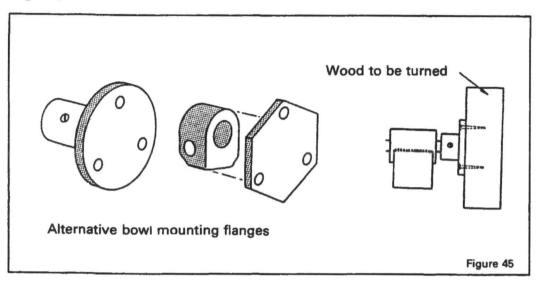

Wood to be turned

Alternative bowl mounting flanges

Figure 45

Position the toolrest about 5 to 10mm from the side of the workpiece. It should not be too far away as the tool would then be difficult to control and might get trapped between the workpiece and the toolrest. Adjust the height of the toolrest so that the tool cuts just above the centre line of the workpiece (Fig. 46).

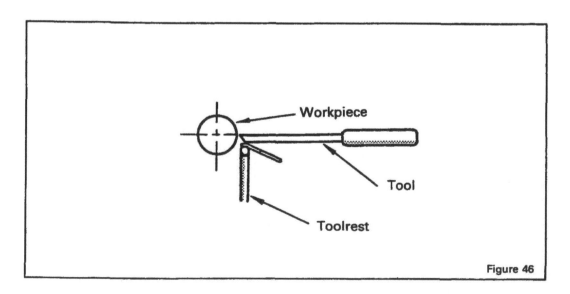

Workpiece

Tool

Toolrest

Figure 46

Adjust the toolrest position inwards as the workpiece diameter decreases, and check the tightness of the tailstock centre every now and then. A small drop of oil or grease on the tailstock centre is useful. Tools should be made of hardened steel, such as is found in old chisels, files or car springs. Some useful tip shapes are shown in Fig. 47.

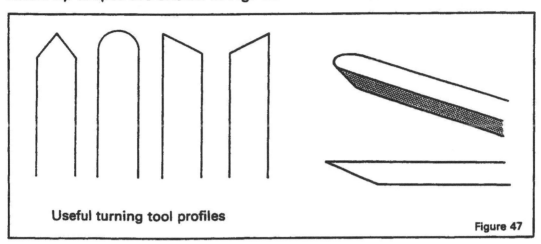

Useful turning tool profiles

Figure 47

Optional designs

If a three-speed hub bicycle wheel is available, it can be used to obtain three cutting speeds. The gears can be changed by pulling the gearchange chain and locking it in place with a piece of 1.6mm plate cut as shown in Fig. 48.

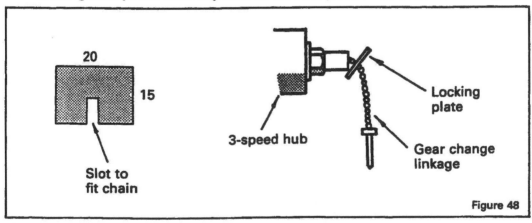

Figure 48

The lathe can be modified to allow a second person to push the treadle, while the lathe operator concentrates on turning the workpiece. The modification involves fitting an extension to the treadle, and a hand-steady to the main beam. The extension could be made from square section MS tube 310 × 25 × 25 (or similar) welded to the treadle in the position shown in Fig. 49. The hand-steady can be made from square section wood turned to a comfortable hand size and attached to the main beam with a wood screw.

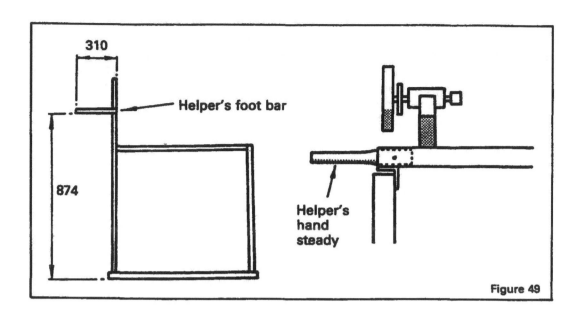

310

Helper's foot bar

874

Helper's hand steady

Figure 49

An electric motor can be fitted to the lathe using a base plate clamped to the stays. Tighten the belt by moving the base plate along the stays and clamping it securely, taking care to line up the pulleys. A shorter drive belt will be needed (Figs. 50 and 51).

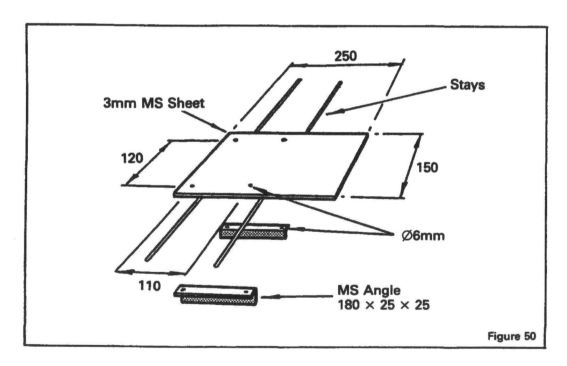

250

Stays

3mm MS Sheet

120

150

Ø6mm

110

MS Angle
180 × 25 × 25

Figure 50

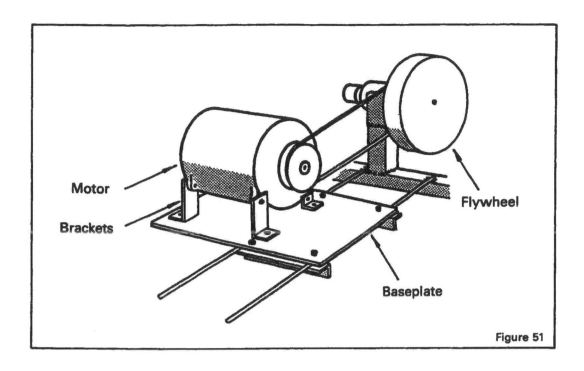

Motor

Brackets

Flywheel

Baseplate

Figure 51

Check list

1. The treadle assembly A should pivot freely around pins A5.
2. The rubber strips A7 must be strong enough to raise the treadle assembly so that the operator can manage a good power stroke.
3. Check that the drive cord E11 is sufficiently tight so that it does not slip on either the bicycle wheel B12 or the pulley C4 (extra turns around the small pulley may help prevent slipping).
4. Power the lathe by operating the treadle; bring it up to working speed. If it vibrates, stop the lathe and re-balance the flywheel C1. The procedure for this is described in the Assembly section.
5. The toolrest assembly D and the tailstock assembly E should slide freely along the main beam B6, when screws D11 and E9 are loose.
6. Ensure that the tool support D2 can be moved so that a cutting tool could be supported at any point along the main beam; it should be possible to swing the tool support out to accommodate a wide workpiece.
7. When all the lock screws are tightened, the tool support should be firm, and should not be free to move at all.
8. Oil all threads, pivots and spindle bearings.